Marine Mammals

Elephant Seals

by Megan Cooley Peterson

Consulting editor: Gail Saunders-Smith, PhD

Consultant: Kathryn A. Ono, PhD
Associate Professor, Department of Marine Sciences
University of New England, Biddeford, Maine

CAPSTONE PRESS
a capstone imprint

Pebble Plus is published by Capstone Publishers,
1710 Roe Crest Drive, North Mankato, MN 56003
www.capstonepub.com

Library of Congress Cataloging-in-Publication Data
Peterson, Megan Cooley.
Elephant seals / by Megan Cooley Peterson.
p. cm.—(Pebble plus. Marine Mammals)
Includes index.
Summary: "Simple text and full-color photographs provide a brief introduction
to elephant seals"—Provided by publisher.
ISBN 978-1-4296-8574-0 (library binding)
ISBN 978-1-62065-312-8 (Ebook PDF)
1. Elephant seals—Juvenile literature. I. Title.

QL737.P64P46 2013
599.79'4—dc23   2012002627

Editorial Credits

Jeni Wittrock, editor; Ted Williams, designer; Svetlana Zhurkin, media researcher; Kathy McColley,
production specialist

Photo Credits

Dreamstime: Sergey Rusakov, cover; Nature Picture Library: Doc White, 17; SeaPics: Bob Cranston, 15, Phillip Colla,
5; Shutterstock: Arto Hakola, 13, Bond967, 7, creativex, 3, Gentoo Multimedia, 21, mcherevan (splash), cover, 1,
Mikhail Dudarev (water texture), cover, 1, Pablo H. Caridad, 19, worldswildlifewonders, 9, 11

Note to Parents and Teachers

The Marine Mammals series supports national science standards related to life science. This
book describes and illustrates elephant seals. The images support early readers in understanding
the text. The repetition of words and phrases helps early readers learn new words. This book
also introduces early readers to subject-specific vocabulary words, which are defined in the
Glossary section. Early readers may need assistance to read some words and to use the Table of
Contents, Glossary, Read More, Internet Sites, and Index sections of the book.

Printed in the United States of America in North Mankato, Minnesota.

042012   006682CGF12

Table of Contents

Hold Your Breath!

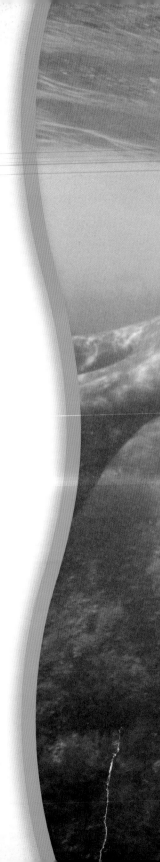

An elephant seal splashes
into the ocean.
This marine mammal needs air
to live. But it can hold its breath
for two hours underwater!

5

Blubber keeps elephant seals warm in icy waters. Northern elephant seals swim in the north Pacific Ocean. Southern seals live in Antarctic waters.

Elephant Seal Range

northern elephant seals

southern elephant seals

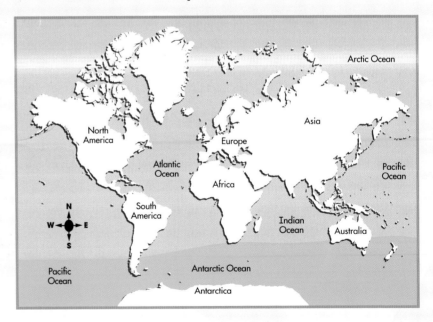

Male elephant seals have noses
that stick out like elephants' trunks.
Males puff up their noses to tell
enemies to stay away.

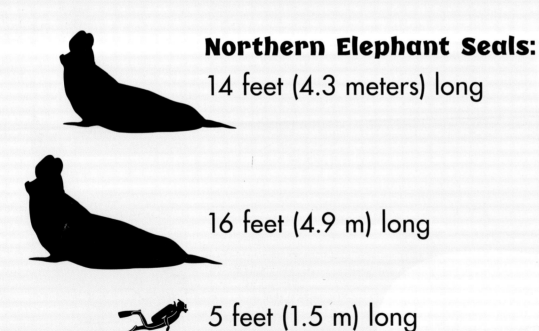

Northern Elephant Seals:
14 feet (4.3 meters) long

16 feet (4.9 m) long

5 feet (1.5 m) long

Hair covers elephant seals' bodies. They molt once a year. Hair and large pieces of dead skin fall off. When molting, they relax in wet sand to calm their skin.

Elephant seals swim through the sea with flippers. On land, they flip cool sand onto their backs with their front flippers. Sand cools them off.

Life at Sea

Elephant seals spend most
of their lives at sea. They hunt
fish, squid, and small sharks.
They dive up to 5,000 feet
(1,500 m) underwater.

Elephant seals spend so much time at sea, they sleep there! When they need air, they swim to the surface. Then the seals slip back underwater to snooze.

Elephant Seal Life Cycle

Southern elephant seals come to shore in September. Northern seals come to shore in December. Females give birth on land to one pup.

Females leave their pups after about one month. Pups teach themselves how to swim and hunt. Elephant seals live about 20 years.

Glossary

blubber—a thick layer of fat under the skin of some animals; blubber keeps animals warm

flipper—one of the broad, flat limbs of a sea creature

hunt—to chase and kill animals for food

mammal—a warm-blooded animal that breathes air; mammals have hair or fur; female mammals feed milk to their young

marine—living in salt water

molt—shedding fur, feathers, or an outer layer of skin; after molting, a new covering grows

pup—a young elephant seal

shore—the place where the ocean meets land

Read More

Goldish, Meish. *Southern Elephant Seal: The Biggest Seal in the World.* More Supersized! New York: Bearport Pub., 2010.

Gray, Susan H. *Elephant Seal.* Road to Recovery. Ann Arbor, Mich.: Cherry Lake Pub., 2008.

Rustad, Martha E. H. *A Baby Seal Story.* Baby Animals. Mankato, Minn.: Capstone Press, 2012.

Internet Sites

FactHound offers a safe, fun way to find Internet sites related to this book. All of the sites on FactHound have been researched by our staff.

Here's all you do:

Visit *www.facthound.com*

Type in this code:1978429685740

Check out projects, games and lots more at
www.capstonekids.com

Index

Word Count: 247
Grade: 1
Early-Intervention Level: 16